MW00991845

ISBN-13 978-1544958620

ISBN-10 1544958625

For my grandchildren

Written by MaryAnn O'Leary
Illustrated by Grace Muchnick

Block Island is a lovely place
With sun and sand and history

Where people come to surf and swim
A place of lore and mystery

Ferry boats and shipwreck tales
Beaches, sailors, pretty shells

Animal farms and bikes to ride

Children jumping in the tide

Flora, fauna, beauty abound

Mopeds make a noisy sound

Lighthouse beacons north and south

Kites, and kayaks, harbors, cows

The island was the home for some

Who built their houses one by one

They lived and worked on sea and land

And many of the homes still stand

When sun sets low on Corn Neck Road

It shines on Captain
Benjamin Gardner's home

The Red House as it now is known
Has frost white trim and stands alone

It was many many years ago
Since the Captain
made this house his home

But now it will forever be known as
The Red House on Corn Neck Road

Made in the USA
Middletown, DE
21 June 2022

67463638R00015